HASTY CORPOREAL INK

HASTY CORPOREAL INK

Lisa Cooper

RESOURCE *Publications* • Eugene, Oregon

HASTY CORPOREAL INK

Copyright © 2024 Lisa Cooper. All rights reserved. Except for brief quotations in critical publications or reviews, no part of this book may be reproduced in any manner without prior written permission from the publisher. Write: Permissions, Wipf and Stock Publishers, 199 W. 8th Ave., Suite 3, Eugene, OR 97401.

Resource Publications
An Imprint of Wipf and Stock Publishers
199 W. 8th Ave., Suite 3
Eugene, OR 97401

www.wipfandstock.com

PAPERBACK ISBN: 979-8-3852-3105-8
HARDCOVER ISBN: 979-8-3852-3106-5
EBOOK ISBN: 979-8-3852-3107-2

VERSION NUMBER 103124

For my dudes.

Contents

Acknowledgements | xi
Introduction | xiii

PART 1: **He informs dew.**

Sunrise Sings | 2
He informs dew | 3
Contemplating Life in the Conservatory | 4
through vale and shallow height | 5
Forging a Sunset | 6
Startle— | 7
Dusk | 8
Waxing Crescent | 9
Insomnia | 10
In the Wintertime | 11
March in New York | 12
Verdant | 13
The Summer Storm that You Slept Through | 15
Autumn | 16
Fall Ends | 17
Unmoved Foundation | 18
The earth's loud weeping | 19
The Branch of Jesse Bears the Tree | 20
The Fear of the Lord Is the Beginning of Wisdom | 22

In Persona Christi | 23
A Firstborn Son | 24
Dear Peter | 25
John 8:36 | 26
The Second Coming | 27

PART 2: **Death is swallowed up in victory.**
Late Nights with You | 30
It didn't have to be this way. | 31
Upon hearing his father died | 32
The Ruins of the Monastery at Oybin | 33
From Ashes to Ashes, Through Water and Fire | 35
Let Your Requests Be Made Known to God | 37
Mourning | 38
She always said lilacs were her favorite | 39
Inheritance | 40
Wishful Dreaming | 41
The Tornado | 42
Abishag the Shunammite | 44
Death is swallowed up in victory | 45
When my grandchildren ask me what the pandemic was like, I'll say: | 46

PART 3: **Memory.**
After the Storm | 48
accelerate | 49
since feeling was first | 50
Leaving | 51
Her smile, then tears | 52
Memory | 53
Unreal | 54
The Look | 55

Studying | 56
Watching Time | 57
January Eighteenth | 58
Son of My Right Hand | 59
Elegy | 60
NYE, NY, NY | 61
Recipe for a Failed Friendship | 62
Grandpa, the Deep Sea Diver | 64
Recess | 65
Sandy Hook | 66
Can Houses Die by Suicide? | 67
Like Mother, Like Daughter | 68
In a boat not my own | 69

PART 4: **Form and Function.**
Form and Function | 72
Insatiable | 73
un-mothering | 74
A Coarse Discourse | 75
Gossip | 76
do his hands cost less? | 77
masculine & feminine | 78
Red Sunset | 79
Get Well Soon | 80
A Vision from the Past | 82
Hasty Corporeal Ink | 83
From Flesh to Flesh | 84
After My Death | 85

Afterword | 87

Acknowledgements

This book would not exist without the love and support of my husband, Jordan. He has been an unfailing source of encouragement in my life—especially in matters like poetry, where I am often hyper-critical of myself. Thank you to Jordan for enduring my late-night poetry rants, reading all my bad poetry drafts, and for finally telling me when it was time to pull the trigger and actually publish this book.

Thank you to my sons, Jacen, and Ben, for helping me select poems for this volume, and for offering insightful critique. They are my favorite people to be creative with. I look forward to the day when I get to see their own work in print.

Thank you to my dad, Richard, for his unencumbered optimism and encouragement in all that I do. I have been immensely blessed to have a father who enthusiastically reads my poems even though he's not really a poetry guy.

Thank you also to my mother, Nancy, for instilling in me a love for poetry from a very young age.

On a more practical level, thank you to Sarah Wisniewski (aka Felto) for copyediting this volume. I can always trust her incredible ability to find and correct any of my errors. Thank you to Michael (Mickey) Haist for allowing me to use his painting for the cover of this volume. I have been a long-time admirer of his paintings, and being able to use one to represent my work is a dream come true.

Thank you also to Wipf and Stock for publishing this volume.

Introduction

When I was in first grade, my teacher had serious Ms. Frizzle vibes. She wore dinosaur shoes and had frizzy, curly hair. As a frizzy-, curly-haired girl myself, we shared a special bond. She was incredible. I don't remember much of my childhood, but I remember her. I remember her oversized glasses. I remember her vibrancy.

It was Christmas time, and I simply had to make her something *worthy*. So, seven-year-old me decided that it would be a perfect idea to test out my computer skills by crafting a stunning clip-art creation. And mind you, this was the era of Windows 95. And I was seven. I had no idea what I was getting myself into.

So, my mother (God rest her soul) sat by my side for hours as I selected a border and various clip-art things. And in the center of the clip-art creation was a poem I wrote for my teacher. It was constructed of cute, rhymed couplets. Something about how I wanted to be like her when I grew up. I wish I could remember more, but it was something like that.

I remember the agony of waiting for this poem to print. It felt like hours. Then it printed in the wrong direction. After fussing with the settings and reworking the page layout, my mom and I finally had my masterpiece ready. My mom bought a frame for it that I subsequently decorated, and we wrapped it as a present for my teacher.

I was so proud. The clip art, the poem, the frame. I felt like a creative genius. And I remember how anticlimactic it felt to

Introduction

actually give it to her. Did she realize how great this gift was? The self-doubt set in, and I felt worried that it would go unappreciated.

But, you know, being seven, I promptly forgot about the whole thing.

Years passed, and I stopped back at my old elementary school and paid her a brief visit. I didn't think she would remember me. If I'm remembering correctly, I was back at the school to teach the third graders how to fold paper cranes. (Why? I don't recall.) Anyway, I stopped by when I was done helping the third-grade class and knocked.

She opened the door to her classroom with a wide smile, turned, and rang a bell. The tiny first graders all convened on a rug at the center of the room that looked like a map of the United States and picked up books to look at.

"Lisa?!" She half-greeted, half-questioned me. She rushed over to her desk and picked up the frame—the one I had forgotten about until that moment. She showed it to me proudly as if to say, "I remember you."

The creation itself was hilarious to look at. The clip art was pixelated, and my poem was silly. But she had kept it. To her, it was more than just a piece of paper with a silly poem on it, created with bad software and printed on my home printer. She saw the value in my efforts, in my words, in my poetry, long before I would.

Poetry has always been a love of mine. I can't remember exactly when it started, but it certainly had something to do with my mom, who was known to write some verses of her own. Hers were always rhymed, always metrical. I admired that. And it definitely had something to do with my local library growing up. I remember going to poetry workshops as a small child and coming home with pages of acrostics and haiku, scrawled in my messy handwriting. I presented them to my dad with the utmost confidence.

I went on to study literature at college, and I never stopped writing poetry. I grew fascinated with the movement of poems, with rhyme schemes, meter, and forms. And the more I read poems written in classic forms, the more I grew disillusioned with what was considered popular, "accessible" contemporary poetry—much

Introduction

of which lacked any markings of what differentiated poetry from regular prose.

In 2019, I challenged myself to write a poem in each of many different traditional forms, and along the way, I became enamored with experimental constraints and all kinds of other interesting ways to bend words to fit into poetic forms. That's when this project began. It became a practice of mine to sit down with a new form, think of a topic that related or worked within the form, and then try my best to bring it to life.

This volume, titled *Hasty Corporeal Ink*, (an anagram of my full name, Lisa Kathryn Cooper) is borne from years of interest and exploration of form and constraint. As I put it together, there were countless hours of counting letters and, embarrassingly, days spent staring at a single *j* and wondering how to make it fit into an anagram. And yet, on the other hand, I awoke with some of these poems in the night, as if they wrote themselves.

Poetry is like football. I know virtually nothing about football, but I know that the people who know about it love it, and the people who don't know anything about it are generally confused and only at the Super Bowl party for the buffalo dip. When you learn the "rules" of poetry, or at least are clued into the "whys," it makes all the difference in the world. Just like when you're watching football. Once you understand the game, no longer are you simply a buffalo-dip-enjoyer, but you can cheer along with your friends and enjoy the game for what it is: a complex, constrained, patterned game governed by rules and signs. Sounds a lot like poetry.

So, this volume is not only this high-flung exploration of poetic form. That would be boring. Rather, it is an invitation for you to peek behind the poetry curtain to see the gears turning. In the back of this book, I've included an afterword. It details the poetic forms and constraints used in each poem. It's an invitation for all who are interested to see the "whys" and "rules" that help shape my own poetry.

As I assembled this book (nine different times, as a poet does), I could see themes emerging: life, death, and everything in

Introduction

between. I will also say before you get to reading that many poems in this volume are written hypothetically. The goal was to make form and function meet in a way that imparts meaning, not necessarily to be true in every regard to my own life. I know a lot of contemporary poetry is highly personal, so I think this caveat needs to be made.

As a Christian, the belief that God ordered the cosmos is fundamental to my faith. And he did it with words. In poetry, there's a unique way in which we—God's creation—can reflect this ordering act with our own words. I hope you enjoy.

In Christ,
Lisa Cooper

PART 1

He informs dew.

Sunrise Sings

The winds of midnight curl beneath the boughs;
they twist, they spiral, flourish, disallow
the moonlight seeking space to catch my eye
from moving past the clouds in darkened sky.
But when the blackness breaks and issues forth
the humming golden aura—from the north
its haze gleams green, a holographic glint
illuminating skyline, coal-gray flint.
From which horizon will the bats take flight?
And where do they go forth to as the night
draws closed? And, folding, from it comes the dawn;
upon the breeze it sings its antiphon:
Glory be to God, whose Word like light
shines bright into the darkness, bringing sight.

He informs dew

Anagram of Proverbs 9:10–12, NKJV

yellow field
yields fine wispy fiber:
Your glory ordinary.

fatuous gold as wisdom
to heathen, woefully
fractured—

for You off lies.

You add beam to leafed wind;
I find You in one lone leaf,

oh,
but arise!
be enlightened!
say,
"Israel, bow to the King;
He informs dew!"

Contemplating Life in the Conservatory

The light gives life to all that lives;
what's living's breath comes forth and we
surround ourselves with all that breathes
and reaches up to meet the light.

What's living's breath comes forth and we
will pluck, will trim, will plant, will weed
that which reaches up to meet the light;
and little hands from womb will learn

to pluck, to trim, to plant, to weed
and growing, too, they live by light,
and little hands from womb will learn
respect for all that grows from soil,

and growing, too, they live by light—
surround themselves with all that breathes—
and respect all that grows from soil,
knowing light gives life to all that lives.

through vale and shallow height

Anagram of Psalm 23, NKJV

how do the steep hills wander and kneel,
reestablished with timeless alms hum?
moon. eye. lengthier praises started:

fondly stir up the meeker heights,
noise soars—
unleash the mess sea-foam shores

through vale and shallow height
i saw You, the cloak of feather dew,
You, a firefly fervor dream,
do You—Trinity—outflow form?
He the oath, my

home.
why are painted beacons lit?
You purveyor of scenery, immune to time;
peel fauna, my prose be herein

frame glory, such life: fruit, whey,
seeds fall tenderly on land
meld—inhale! love!
hallowed is the Lord of wooly moss!

Forging a Sunset

The molten metal pools within the mold,
and red-hot iron will flash with hammer's strike.
Sparks fly abreast and rest by skyline's fold,
while wet-deep darkness wrenches downward light
to sleep—beneath horizon cooled to touch.
What once was light refracting 'round the sun,
striations of the evening, groping, clutch,
as moonbeam's marble renders skyline numb.
The furnace of the day, a stifled glow—
extinguished till the work resumes anew;
yet all at once the thousand starlights show,
breaking forth through blackened nighttime's hue.
The Maker rests, His daily work complete.
And comforted, the calmed creation sleeps.

Startle—

The birds have gone silent;
sensation held—bright eve,
native threshing bees, old
beings. The love-tarnished
stars die; high, noble event,
and in sight, beetles hover
beneath, thrive. Godliness
beat; no light-shred in eves,
doth evening reestablish:
disaster be the novel nigh:
the birds have gone silent.

Dusk

When the whole whale-road
turned timidly to tinsel-shade,
and night-blanket nestled near
into the inmost inches—
I thanked the Tapestry-weaver,
the Wise-man who watches
while sky-tears shimmer down sparkling,
as if all angels cried
beautiful water-beads bearing light.
Neither kings nor noblest men
can conduct a coastline's ripple,
and bend the black depths back like He.
But He who hears from heaven
the tumultuous tantrum of sin-tears
restores and redeems the wrongful sighs,
and places a sweet sparkle on the sea.

Waxing Crescent

Can you see his palms unfurl the night,
resisting weight of humid air like glass?
Encased around his skin, the beads at last
spring forth from bark and drop from highest height.
Cascading down, his tears, they fall from sight.
Enter while you can beneath its mass.
Nocturnal creatures, plodding through the grass,
tell stories of the birch till morning bright.

When all is darkened, sparkle still the stars.
Arise the glistening moonlight, shrouded, slim;
X-ray birds depart from heavenly perch
into the pools of obscure light, ajar.
Nothing seems to meet us here, but limb—
grotesque, disfigured fingers of the birch.

Insomnia

When I awake to
moonlight's softness through curtains,
a flickering beam,

its brilliance like ice
refracted upon the walls—
I watch its stars dance;

with eyes open to
the show, I can't stop watching.
There's no need for sleep.

In the Wintertime

In the wintertime all of creation
lies silent, a glittering foundation.
The sun from above sets over the snow,
casting long shadows and a golden glow.
We should rightly respond: adoration.

To whom do we address this ovation?
Whose handiwork deserves veneration?
The God who gives abundantly, we know
in the wintertime.

My boy's hand holding mine, pure elation;
a cloud escapes his lips—exhalation.
Bending his arm with a snowball to throw,
his target ahead with eyes all aglow:
happiness of a new generation
in the wintertime.

March in New York

The willows wear white dresses;
crocuses veil, crowd in crisis—
shocked with snow, as searing cold
billows, breezes over blasted path.
Icicles inch, long, into fingers
which, frantic, feel the forsythia flowers'
dainty petals and pinch perforations;
bruised but not broken, the bloodroots bleed,
extend, reaching with riotous rigor
toward the towering sun; together
with windflower, they wane not, wilt not.
Yet with the warm light's washing waves,
unfolding from frost, they fan, fragrant,
and boldly burst with bare beauty.

Verdant

Kelly, among the ferns, lay down
and spotted a mantis praying.
Her army boots were wet, dirt-brown;
paintbrush treetops with wind swaying.

The horizon whispered its pines,
and echoed its maples: sap brimmed,
spilled its paleness from deep confines,
poured into bucket, fully rimmed.

In the grove, a jungle of buds
and moss. Standing now, and sipping,
tea from hunter canteen floods
her mouth. Standing now, and dripping,

she peers through the misty forest:
the picture transfigured jade—leaves
and grass—light and emerald nourished,
shimmering with morning dew, weaves

up, down length of towering height.
And could it be the scent of mint
in the air? Was the ground in sight
peeling back, revealing a hint

as an avocado peels back
brown, with its verdant guts beneath?
Bright Kelly among the deep black,
and algae rimming the brook, breathes—

her boots now set aside, and feet
dipped in—clover beneath fingers,
cool, shallow water lapping, and sweet
dappled forest where she lingers.

The Summer Storm that You Slept Through

The unrelenting pattering of rain—
it drummed and rapped and tapped and loud! The sky
has opened up, bursting, a dark freight train;
it howled, rumbled, echoed thunder cry;

it drummed and rapped and tapped. And loud, the sky:
all bright for an instant, then went pitch dark;
it howled, rumbled, echoed thunder cry,
but all is darkness. Yet, a single spark:

all bright for an instant, then went pitch dark;
so I leaned over, kissed your sleeping eyes.
Still all is darkness, yet a single spark
awoke all nature, swirling in the skies.

When I leaned over, kissed your sleeping eyes,
outside it grumbled low, a dark freight train
awoke all nature, swirling in the skies:
the unrelenting pattering of rain.

Autumn

A presence suddenly gripped—
my eyes focused on the door:
her fingertips slowly peeked red
around the maple wood.

With a forcible swoop
of her carnelian hand-span,
the door swung open;
cascading curls, auburn ringlets:
the light about her refined a halo
of molten gold.

A certain smell hung about her,
and her apple-tree lips laughed
a cool breeze; a pleasant chill
shot up my spine—Ah!
to breathe the air of a
new world touched by that same hand,
a new world speckled in
her paintbrush precision.

She smoldered:
the early setting sun
revealed her deep, smooth, earth-shade eyes.
Were they not the same color as the
deepest soil ever dug?—almost black,
and as rich with life?

Fall Ends

the trees dappled
deep red maples
the leaves shine bright
a thread the light

to whirl around
spun gold melts down
and wraps dispels
'round old church bells

winds hear its sound
the pine sings out
it's sharp the cold
and lines thresholds
    blur when
        fall ends

Unmoved Foundation

Anagram of Hebrews 4:12, NKJV

grip the root
of stronghold and rip—
wear the first fjord
of wooded vision,
changed in an instant.

configures then-fated
harsh air whistles, whips,
adopts rearview tint:

an unmoved foundation
needs no added glory

The earth's loud weeping

The earth's loud weeping wet its war-stained brow,
and fires of discontentment lit the night.
And stomping still, its trudging with the plow
dragged on and on upon the earth's cruel blight,
its mantle heavy, hardened by the hail.
Distressed, it wrest the anger from its breast
and beat its bonds, then shouted loud its wail!
The feeble voice of fear expressed, confessed.
Then arches of church windows bent the light
to bind with particles strewn through the air,
refracting emerald green, the cross a kite—
which lifted eyes to heaven, sins to bear.
The whole of heaven, halcyon, can't contain
such grace that falls afresh like hallowed rain.

The Branch of Jesse Bears the Tree

The Branch of Jesse bears the tree,
Golgotha-bound to set us free.
Jerusalem where prophets die,
True Lamb of God silent complies;
He wanted more than anything
To gather them under His wing.

The Son of God whose lonely road
Was paved with sweat and blood which flowed.
The purple robe had been removed,
His body torn and badly bruised.
Plod on toward death, the cross's weight
Simon of Cyrene helped abate.

The Word of God who formed the earth
Heard His creation gloat with mirth;
As Craftsman of the World dragged on,
The nearby women mourned aloud
And criminals on either side
Walked with Him to be crucified.

The Son of Man bids us to go
And carry crosses of our own.
As gathered in His name, all tribes
Look to His suffering as our guide.
And, as He promised, He will come
Again one day on clouds above.

True Priest and King, true Sacrifice
Stayed on the path to make wrong right;
And when we face what brings us fear,
Let us with confidence draw near
Close to our Lord in times of strife:
Our dreadful burden He makes light.

The Fear of the Lord Is the Beginning of Wisdom

When will the wrath of God come near?
I worry late with hands outspread.
"In Jesus Christ there is no fear,"

the preacher said with boldness, cheered
but followed close with warning dread:
"Stave off the wrath of God, come near;

so work, work hard!" He warned, "Adhere
perfectly to the law," he said,
but Jesus Christ—he took that fear.

In-bodied man, God volunteered
to bear all wrath on his own head,
and when the wrath of God came near

the weight of sin, it lay and seared
His flesh. He died there in our stead.
In Jesus Christ there's no more fear—

now no one needs to shed a tear,
and wonder idly on their bed,
"When will the wrath of God come near?"
Because in Jesus there's no fear.

In Persona Christi

"Let us arise!" Celebrant
donned his thick vestments, boldly
to the gold cup elegant
went, lifting his hands slowly.

He placed them on elements,
pronounced the words with vigor—
held and shook the evidence
of eternal life secure

as though he was heaven-sent.
He stood there in his disguise
in stead of Christ—testament—
God's mercy, let us arise!

A Firstborn Son

His body folded, knees up to his chest;
his tiny face held sweetly in my hand.
A son was born, and I am richly blessed,
and for this boy, I now know love firsthand.

So how did God the Father turn away
when Jesus, his own son, was forced to die?
The Father's holy justice on display,
while perfect Lamb, God's wrath would satisfy.

I scarcely know such love, but know in part;
it terrifies the soul of every man
who knows their child and hears their beating heart—
and all of this to finish God's whole plan

against sin, the devil, death, and his allies.
The Son that day his love did surely prove;
through pain and anguish, terror shook the skies.
His final cry: *"They know not what they do."*

Dear Peter

I am not here, Peter. Please promise
in the morn while sounds combine
and—loud—cries morrow rooster,
turn, tears, repent.

I to the hill climb: bright Calvary!
My arm bent, heavy burden bearing.
But, your Guide, unlike earthly
king, cries. Afraid somehow, bleeding—

I am not here, Peter. Please provide
my own with bread always. Imagine:
you feed sheep abroad, nourish
them while broken.

I am the King whose church
is the true light.
And your gifts,
dear Peter, matter.

John 8:36

Though in transgression, God won't leave me be;
though lost, defeated, and in sin I died,
the Love of God comes near to set me free.

From in the pew, my sins shown plain to me,
My soul—tormented—tries to run and hide;
though in transgression, God won't let me be

left picking, eating fruit from that damned tree,
left to my own devices, tricks, and lies.
The Love of God comes near to set me free.

Though bleeding, pleading, down on bended knee;
the Law of God demands I pay a price—
though in transgression, God won't leave me be.

God became flesh, the God-man, one and three,
to ransom the whole earth of every vice;
the Love of God came here and set us free!

Now given to us, His body by decree,
His blood, forgiveness, more than any prize.
Though in transgression, God won't leave us be;
the Word of God came near and set us free.

The Second Coming

Puffs erupt—round, full eclipsing cornrows, towering.
Eager, rapt faces engrossed; can the piping,
resounding fanfare epiphany capture the profound encounter?
Flee! Exalt! Crawl toward places exposed. Raise
eyes cloud-ward, trumpets piercing. Elated ringing, flaring!
Can the pearlescent eves—radiant—feel encounters
this perfect? Enlightened, reflective, flawless—enormous calm.

PART 2

Death is swallowed up in victory.

Late Nights with You

"There's things that bind and things that slowly break,"
you said. Enumerating loss, we count—
I hope to God this isn't a mistake,

with every word, such sorrow, such heartbreak—
you felt the words around you, stuck. You doubt
that thing that binds, while things, they slowly break.

While thinking here, your vanity must make
decision firm to plant, to grow, to sprout,
and hope to God this won't be a mistake.

Sprung forth from ashes, you must now forsake
all other sounds, the contrary accounts
of things that bind. Yet things that slowly break

keep piling all around you now and shake;
they fall, broken yet again—it amounts
to hope. Pray "God, this isn't a mistake."

Remind yourself of this while wide awake
in bed: your time has still not yet run out
of things that bind and things won't always break,
so, comfort now—this isn't a mistake.

It didn't have to be this way.

The fractals of her lipstick on cup's rim,
and sweetened air still lingered near her room.
Her cursive, looping, swooping, inked through lines
on pad of paper strewn in her bedroom.

I looked for her by couch near windowpane—
then there, the precipice of nevermore—
I squinted through the fog of memory,
but saw that still there's nothing to look for:

the remnants of a meal, a fork, a spoon,
and shaken salt still peppered countertop;
a light left buzzing loud, grown strangely dim,
then footsteps, quiet, came to halting stop.

The hallway rug ran straight to bathroom's door;
her cheek was cold and pressed on tiled floor.

Upon hearing his father died

When, long ago, death was a far-off thing,
and what was I? A flitting ghost of me
whose body, mind, and spirit came to blows
so as to project the proper person. Pained,
the voice I heard the former night was soft
as glass that shattered, tearing deep his face—

reeling forward, where I shook confused, wrung
my hands together like an alien skin.
I felt the tickle in my throat, was it
that laughter rising—bubbled, almost choked;
I strained to fight its gurgle with a frown
and furrowed brows to make me clearly sad.

Who was this girl held tightly in my skin?
And why the smile, the obvious lack of care?
The Ferris wheel of anger turned inside
to find the right emotion for the job.
But how does one respond to tragedy
with nothing of a repertoire of words?
Who can teach the skill, the genuine craft,
of hearing of a death with open ears?

The Ruins of the Monastery at Oybin

Soft and swift, the pale light sews,
and tracing through the terrace, glows
with blossomed rays through brick and by
filigrees float then frightened fly
away from wreckage woefully wrought
and, turning, tracing careful thought:

I ponder this, then, trembling thought,
would this willow willingly sow
on stone, by window lonely wrought
with fraying branch, though buds still glow
with life, forgotten? Ferns and flies
hover, hem and hum nearby;

they greet the breeze blown gently by
and think not on that terrible thought
of abandoned abbey flying
through time and temperament, it sews
in vain its vaults still empty glow
with nothing, no one, nowhere wrought

more waste. But windows, willing, wrought
a vision: beauty beaming by.
A hill away, with hope then glows
with courage: country canyon thought
that temple taken by time sews
alone through nature, so we fly

there with our vision, float like flies
or eagles, with wings that wrought
such wind, from sky we sow
and bid the monastery goodbye
and give it not another thought,
since breath and life beyond would glow.

Yet dangling from its death, now glows
the phantom halls now full, songs fly
and echo, loud engulfed with thoughts
and animate again, and wrought
with verbose voices, by and by
and singing psalter, hope is sown.

The building glows with beauty wrought
with light. They fly through doorway, by
their simple thoughts, new life is sown.

From Ashes to Ashes, Through Water and Fire

Your body, Mom,
    was burned in a shock
        of red and yellow,
swept into piles,
    and entombed in tin.
        There I held you again.

What's left of you
    I carefully placed,
        leaning over the edge
of the steep
    walkway overlooking
        the falls.

What's left of you:
    softly sprinkled,
        then rushing
down in
    bubbling, moving
        water.

From here,
    looking down,
        you are caught
on rocks,
    and transformed in
        foam.

Mom, will God sweep your
    scattered bits and,
        with his gentle fingers,
piece each atom together?
    Will he know where you
        live now with no gravestone?

You loved this
    churning spot.
        Mom, I cannot
remain here
    forever, but
        you will—until that day.

Let Your Requests Be Made Known to God

Anagram of Philippians 4:6–7, NKJV

Ashen fixations
give way to yearning,
and yearning to
tired throngs—
a battalion brought
sounding lungs,
weeping with
curly, knotted prayer;
numbered arsenal with
quivers, poised to
cut.
Hush! Shh.
Hands pick
up crumbled
shards of gold:
Jesus.

Mourning

come
to me
with no breath,

and no words.
silently hold
me.

She always said lilacs were her favorite

I clipped the lilac sprigs, stems thick in hand:
thin, delicate pink chasms swell—expand.
Her cheeks dim lit, distant in photos tacked
upon the board above her ashes packed

into a tin that seemed too small to fit
her body. So confusing—white and grit.
The scent of flowers carried in the air,
bloomed, lingered there, as if my silent prayer.

Inheritance

As I place the bracelet,
    adjust the closure and hear
it snap, fastened
    and loose around my wrist,
        I thank her.

As I run my fingers over diamonds:
    shining braille formed from
the depths of the earth—
    fracturing light around my wrist,
        I tell her I miss her.

As I look down
    and see a hand unrecognizable,
glittering with gold, and white orbs
    that shine out, a regal statement on my wrist,
        I whisper to her:

—*this shouldn't be mine just yet.*

Wishful Dreaming

She does not come to me in dreams,
but in my dreams, she is alive;
I smell her scent upon the breeze,
but she never does arrive.

I walk and walk the winding stage
of houses, buildings, people, kids;
I turn and turn the phonebook page
to find the place where she now lives:

each name is small, each number too;
I finally find her new address,
but at her door I peer inside:
nothing. Resounding emptiness.

I visited every church that day
trying to spot her wavy hair,
to see her singing in the choir,
but I couldn't find her there.

Still does my mother run from me,
or does she know she's gone for good?
I swear I smelled her scent: alive!
Perhaps I misunderstood.

Why would she hide in dreams from me?
She could tell me I've been all wrong—
that she didn't die by suicide
but an accident after all.

The Tornado

The blue-green light shone forth in darkened room,
illuminated—barely—both of us;
our eyes grew wide as news of horror scene:
the wind, the trees, the displaced body parts
came into view. Houses crumpled paper,
roads gave way to water, concrete pieces,

cars dissected into fallen pieces,
the inside of each house exposed, each room;
walls which held the bits of smiling paper,
framed, were broken—portraits like ones of us,
as unaffected anchors read their parts:
their "breaking news" in monotone, the scene,

not unlike rehearsed play, a practiced scene,
swirling, where the set was splayed in pieces,
actors loudly shouted their feeble parts.
I glanced at you, still seated, in our room
as a great chasm lengthened between us.
The stern anchorwoman read from paper,

startled, she, shaking, lowered the paper,
as she told the story—a family's scene,
we listened as if it were about us:
"Their house began to fall into pieces;
the mom and daughter hid in the bathroom.
The little girl, still made of all soft parts,

could hardly stand against the crumbling parts,
as walls fractured, pipes ruptured, and paper
peeled from the walls, and even the bathroom
became something from a film—a bleak scene
of bloodied bodies, blown into pieces."
You insisted that, if this had been us,

as human shield, you'd have protected us.
Even if your body were ripped to parts,
I'd have crawled out from under your warm pieces—
A hero! You'd appear in every paper,
as I, a small girl, would recount the scene,
but we're barely alive in this dark room.

Failing, our family in pieces, and us,
in this room together, rehearsed each part:
Bacardi, shredded paper, sullen scene.

Abishag the Shunammite

The cold creeps up, I feel it in my bones;
her hair is soft, she holds me like a robe.
She looks upon my frailty and—sweet—
her hands of duty wrap my hands and feet.
While, rabid dog, my son fights for the throne
and bids to make the lovely girl his own,
her hands prepare me, gently, for the grave;
her eyes cast down, and carefully she staves
away my fears. I touch her hair so smooth
as cold embraces, she has power to soothe.

Death is swallowed up in victory

Anagram of 1 Corinthians 15:54, NKJV

run! the Physician has made
death burn,
wove saints a garment
tightly—tools
to withstand rot;
unspools limp sin-torn city,
all without
prior wrath,
but establishes
rich hope upon it

When my grandchildren ask me what the pandemic was like, I'll say:

I think we loved death then. I think we do
still think of her when quiet nighttimes fall;
silence attends the movement of our sheets,
reaching for her but finding none at all.

Her calm, patient, quiet resilience won
as stifled heartbeats muffled, lungs gave way,
and people looked in anger, watched the news
on ways to keep her deadliness at bay.

But anger seethed and, fraught with displaced rage,
the people lost the battle—lost their breath.
Hundreds of thousands dead by first year's end;
those left alive still whisper her name: death.

She made herself known only as she passed,
a slow, soft noise like silence feared and gasped.

PART 3

Memory.

After the Storm

The pines stretched out to reach the weeping sky,
and yet this storm has passed, our footsteps wet
and caked with mud; we'll get there by and by,

but with each step, I pray you'll soon forget
how loud my heartbeat shouted as we kissed;
the rushing of the water a quartette—

a haunting tune—the anguish of our tryst,
it overwhelmed my senses, shook my bones;
so how then did you hear, and still resist?

I wonder to myself with each small stone…
The sticky haze surrounded as we went,
and with each step I step into unknown.

So sir, my dear, as we make our descent,
I pray that soon you'll make clear your intent.

accelerate

accept my apologies, sweetie;
can a man who runs ever stop? Can't
count on a bullet to halt, extra
evenings groaning again. It's you—your
longing eyes always make the eerie
echo on my way out linger. I'll set all
readiness aside. I'll stand idle
around the staircase, stare and panic,
then falter again. I'll stay—manic;
exposed, unsettled, as we make this idea

accelerate

since feeling was first

after e e cummings, "since feeling is first"

since feeling was first
he had studied her lines, and
rehearsed with his tongue
a want of bodily wisdom and wished

—the base of her neck flickered warm
with dappled light,

let his eyes fall rapt
on her unbuttoning;
autumnal bodies are soft
full of disruptive feeling:

a whole kiss in exchange for
all my forever small moments
but i swear by all beamed light

the movement of his
calloused sunrise hands
can augment all feeling,
render the fat of her thighs
to suppleness

i think alone,
no arms, no weight of presence
no feeling
but the heaviness of loss

Leaving

The sunlight was blurring as your pastels
smudged out around tree branches, bleak.
And out in the distance, I heard the bells
toll out, hovering over the creek.

Icicles forming out on the porch
drip down, shimmering out in the cold.
The firelight glowing out from my torch
waxed, waned, flickering out, growing old.

Persistent, the sky still pushed forth its light;
your canvas began to grow dim,
and, parting the clouds, ushered forth the night.
Your countenance, likewise, was grim.

With sobering silence, you grabbed your things,
packed up with not even a word.
Dark birds above rustled, flapping their wings;
your leaving was quiet, unheard.

I looked at the sunset, watched you depart.
Our time here was surely too brief.
But foraging here for our thoughtful art,
though short, was a welcome relief.

Her smile, then tears

The happiest love poems still always end—
spot and appease—he wills loveliest myth;
it seamlessly happened at hilltops, wove
past epitaphs. Will to many loveless heed

the wisdom that what's here could all be gone;
welcomed true hollows—that height and base
dwell, saw that he too blushed; come in, gather
courage. He hid hollowness, battled what met

him there as idle strain longing for her breath.
Bonding heart, flesh into arms; hear either girl,
regal and light, breathe in shore forms, inherit
original bond. Fresh, right. Her smile, then tears

Memory

There's nothing small in memory
that I would like to change,
and nothing still would make me whole
about thinking on the exchange.

Yes, years have passed, and I remain
the same one that you left—
yet, years it's been since I've been here
and years since I, bereft,

thought on that night when you had gone,
descending the staircase;
the starlight painted blue and gold
the angles of your face.

Nostalgia is a bitter tool;
it wars against my will.
It dulls the memory I have,
and paints it glowing still.

Quiet, nostalgia! I have screamed,
please let me go to sleep!
Please close my eyes to memory,
and let me, happy, keep

my love, my life, and all things good
that newly are my own.
And let me rest in happiness,
now that happiness I've known.

Unreal

Did I catch feelings?
When you
pulled and kissed—
I melted.

Something strange,
unreal.

Strange—something melted;
I kissed and pulled
you.
When feelings catch:

I did.

The Look

if I could teach you the language of
              when I lift my eyes and blink, just barely,
"The Look," if you will,
              you could know exactly what I'm thinking
as we sit here in this loud bar;
              I wouldn't have to read your lips, wet
with your head down, folded hands,
              with concerned anticipation:
what would happen next?
              is this band too loud?
I can see your breath ripple your drink,
              an exhaled thought, but
I could teach you my language
              you could learn the movement of my lips,
but you'd have to *want* to notice the signs
              and look up, maybe once, from your drink

Studying

The way you stroke your beard with your hand
with that look of consternation,
the way your eyebrows furrow
when you're concentrating;
I love all these things
and much, much more
if only
you could
see.

Watching Time

He started collecting watches,
wide watches with
thin hands ticking time,
and yet with each second,
we come a moment closer to
till death do us part,
and I watch the anxiety on his face.

January Eighteenth

Hear the tiny heir
his yearn, a high grunt.
Ahh, tear nutrient-thin teat
inane trying—rung.
Trite taunt thy teeth to
tether, tug here and
earn thine grain. At night teary,
hear thy injury.
Reign! Rage! Hair and grit
yet ruin—yearning
hurt, unearthing energy
uneaten. I try
yet tire. Reunite
near and hunt: retain
thy genuine gaiety
eat thy treat herein.

Son of My Right Hand

Mere heat of hands would melt the chocolate kiss—
a thought that passed, but frivolous, dismissed;
he dug his hands far deeper, shoved his palm
into his pockets as he ran to mom.
A melted mess, his sticky hands would hold
her face, his fingers smearing, and behold!
His mom, whose gaze engaged from eyes to eyes,
scooped the child up and reeling, he capsized
upon the couch. And, laughing still, she kissed
the chubby fingers, sweetened, as they gripped
her pillows, fabric, face, her nails, her skin—
his squeals of joy erupted with his grin.
The days of sticky fingers surely close,
and open others wide as child grows.

Elegy

In quiet mornings when I stir, awake:
a stretch, a blink—I miss your dreamy mild.
The comfort of your warmth, untethered, free;
I know that one day you'll return to me.

I dreamt of calmness, sitting by the lake,
but woke, disrupted by a restless child;
please come back softly, this my ardent plea
in quiet mornings when I stir awake.

In bleary unrest, I can scarce conceive
a world in which my mind would wake alert,
and hopeful toward the hours left of day.
A stretch, a blink—I miss your dreamy mild:

the low hum, rumble, of a passing train,
the almost-silence of the ceiling fan.
And wrapped up tight, I closed my eyes and slept;
the comfort of your warmth, untethered, free.

In midst of loss, I weep for loss of thee—
your speechless softness was my sure comfort.
And yet a time when these small ones are grown,
I know that one day you'll return to me.

NYE, NY, NY

The dim-lit evening bent beneath the clouds,
full-formed and fluffed atop the buildings sat;
I stood in such a way to take less space
and sucked up air through nostrils quietly.

Yet, upside down, a detailed nighttime scene
was lengthened, the dark city glowed pastel.
The mob of ruffled tourists snub and flit;
dispassionate, they tout their alcohol.

From labyrinth of darkened doors and drapes,
the halo city lights intensified,
as alien eyes peered out into the night,
and crowds of bodies swayed from side to side.

But with a flash! The edges of my view
went purple, crashing loud—a screaming halt—
then voices raised to loud and able chorus,
greeting the new year with pulsing lights.

And up above, the streaking fireworks banged,
which, loosening their gritty drops of ash,
descended on us as a flaky snow.
I brushed away the manna of the night

as it clung to squinting eyelids' lashes.
Percussive noises shook inside my chest
and echoed 'round the sea of bodies on
cold concrete. Our breath was vapor rising.

Recipe for a Failed Friendship

Step One:
Take two hearty shakes of long distance and combine well with a cup of different beliefs. Beat on high for ten years until tripled in size.

Step Two:
Gently fold in the different friends, places, and passions neither of us will share with each other. Sprinkle in tragedy, death, and chronic illness—careful not to deflate the hot air that's built up in the mix.

Step Three:
In a separate bowl, stir together two separate cities, five states, two kids, seven different jobs, and two marriages between us. Combine with little sleep, no words to share, and working too much.

> Optional: Add four consecutive years of "Happy Birthday!" texts exchanged, three attempted group photos, and one "I miss you" text, left unread.

Step Four:
Combine all ingredients in one large bowl, then spoon generously into a tin and bake for four evenings of frustrated conversation—talking past one another—two lonely coffee dates, one social media miscommunication, and two catastrophic, divisive elections.

Step Five:
Remove from heat and let stand at room temperature in silence

for five months. Top with that pit-in-your-stomach longing, four drags of one shared cigarette in a noisy crowd of strangers, and one awkward hug goodbye.

Step Six:
Repeat.

Grandpa, the Deep Sea Diver

The swirling deeps, the sun, the rocking boat
atop the tide like fragrance on the wind;
the smell of salt, a sheen, a sticky coat—
the depths I've yet un-plunged, the darkness rimmed.
I peer into the water, cold as death;
I think about him, lunged as other men,
who wanted to inhale—pull one last breath
through hose through tube through tank—and gasp again.
To hold his hand that met the sea with courage,
to kiss the stubble of his cheek once wet,
to dance together on the deepest stage—
I'd let him pull me close, but we've not met.
I wonder if he'd recognize me here;
forevermore, I look at waves and fear.

Recess

I sharpened fingernails to dagger points
and painted the tips white to show their length,
flashed the cruel weapons as I stroked my hair:
a warning to the brood my mounting strength.

And that day without warning I would strike,
protrusions like a knife dug out their skin
sore, bleeding, they cried loud—the rest would leave
behind my brother, frazzled with his chin

hung low so I could barely see his tears.
"Retarded!" they called out, and I would curse
and raise my fist to threaten, spit in dirt.
His voice broke as I picked him up; what's worse

is that I didn't help at all. It'd be
that damage caused was more than I could see.

Sandy Hook

This boy I love, heart beating in his chest,
awoke that morning, kissed my cheek goodbye—
will breathe no more, breath stolen from his breast.

His hair all tangled as he slowly dressed,
he squinted at me with the bluest eyes.
This boy I love, heart beating in his chest;

I placed my hand upon his head, caressed
his mane of curls, silky, soft, and high.
He breathes no more, breath stolen from his breast.

The bullets rained down, as they all attest;
I fix his face before me as I cry:
"My boy's small heart was beating in his chest!"

This monster took his gun and firmly pressed
the trigger toward himself—we can't know why
he breathes no more, breath stolen from his breast.

Years have gone since I laid my boy to rest;
I cannot think of him with eyes still dry;
this boy I love—heart beating in his chest—
will breathe no more, breath stolen from his breast.

Can Houses Die by Suicide?

She opened up her doors, embraced it all:
the murky sewage water stank of piss,
and silently it seeped in through the walls,
but this small house was once a lovers' bliss.

You see, these lovers here, they had it all:
a house, two kids, a dog, and all of that.
Yet the house—despised—sought an end, to fall
into this ocean head-long: death at last!

Her last small breaths, strained, muffled by the mold
grown in her bloodline, deep beneath the boards.
Her shutters agape, cringing at the cold;
left destitute. Is this what love affords?

Although her spirit's gone, the home remains
as love abounds and pulses through their veins.

Like Mother, Like Daughter

I saw the twisted wringing of her hands;
the thin blue veins sat veiled beneath her skin.
Weathered, worn, and wasted were her words,
but I, my dear, ran quickly from her sin.

But who can blame a woman such as her,
whose vices were no product of her own?
Whose hands, however, brought the poison near
to burn her lips, but she could not atone—

her hands that pushed, that dug deep bloody nails,
(violence described in sullen, soft, hushed tones)
but piercing screams did nothing to deter
that man with evil eyes and rotting bones.

—I pushed aside all thoughts of her from me:
those sad depictions of a mother scorned.
When she spoke, her sadness leeched from her,
but I, my dear, could not be so forlorn.

Until that night I learned just how it felt
to be gripped and wrestled, pinned and raped—alone,
wrenching my red wrists from grasping hands;
her quiet nervous tick became my own.

In silent rooms, she never heard me speak
of what transpired on those bleak white sheets.
I could not discern her eyes, nor thoughts behind;
but she looked at me, she touched my face, and sighed.

In a boat not my own

A rented boat would keep myself afloat;
I paddled alone till the break of dawn
exhausted, leaning forward, tightened throat.
Press on! I said to me, you must press on!
From there, the sunrise looked like flowing curls,
with ringlets falling light upon the waves;
the shining looked as if a string of pearls
was wrapped around what water still remains
between the land and me, a chasm still
was filled with longing, long was there to go.
Yet how was I, a smart girl, to distill
the meaning behind all that was below—
I could have drowned, that could have been my last…
but suffering, I lived and lived steadfast.

PART 4

Form and Function.

Form and Function

Find a random draft, and—
frantic—turn a form.
Trim and confirm: no
daft rant found.
Don a font, and coin
a fount of info;
unfit manic id
and infant fact.
A foundation uniform:
a format of art.

Insatiable

Abstain in Lent,
absent bestial ties
set to lean tines in—
abate its banal bites.
        Nail it. Net it.
Ban Satan: slain beast.
Insatiable sin be silent!

un-mothering

a bygone child dances,
elated, for God;
He, in jubilant kindness,
lifts mine near onto
peaceful, quiet resting spot—
there undoes violent wishes,
explains youthful zeal.
your xanax-woman
visits—undone—the
sterile receded quarters,
praying over nausea;
mothering like
kaleidoscope joy inhibited,
hurricane grief
festering each day;
come back again

A Coarse Discourse

I yell
a spell
to ward
off horde
and group
my troop
to slay—
obey;
I brew
what drew
this craze:
a phrase,
words keen
and mean.

Gossip

A
hi
is

fit
for
gab;

cede
facts,
make
joke.

Dance—
eager
irony-
laced
gaffe

—deafen
truths,
abject
schema:
making
gossip.

do his hands cost less?

Anagram of Psalm 82, NKJV

do his hands cost less
than your eroded hateful jaws—
open hole with unshakeable threats
see that withered orphan suffocate...
what if had I said I enjoyed it
and nodded darkly with you

would you tighten my unbound infection,
graft the bone as my teeth grind;
could you still knowingly
hear of all disoriented fear and jeer?

let me, failing, stagger to Golgotha hill,
choked and knotted in my guts,
headache deep in head.
please look from on high,
Holy God, feed us lost
and to font gather;
refresh us unhealthy, oh Lord,
join tenderly to me Defender,
content just like a father, love a son

masculine & feminine

morning stood still &
a sound, a touch of
sunlight when he
came in, though I'm
uneasy—unsure if I
like this. green
inseam split-tangle; I
negotiate, trim in.
endless, I end it and flee—

Red Sunset

The fires of night begin their glow, deep red;
with dim refracted light, the sky reaps red.

The river Dnipro is a sea of rust,
or tea; it darkened with the time, steeped red.

I hear the ringing of alarms again,
and looking out, the singing bombs weep red.

Each movement of my eyes disrupts the dust;
upon my eyelids ashes sleep. Red

still, as the sun awakes, it brings forth blood;
the clouds, my hands, inside—it all seeps red.

The world aflame, yet still more strangely cold;
what's lost is lost, and burning still bleak-red.

Get Well Soon

My daughter buckles in her fits of rage,
convulses with her legs, arms, teeth, and nails.
Her friend from school with glowing deep brown eyes
wants more than all to play with daughter's toys.

So daughter grasped the building block and threw—
it soared above the pristine plush white rug.
A strike! It landed, peeling back the skin,
and blood poured forth from daughter's friend's fresh wound.

Wailing, her flesh was raw, the cut ran deep:
the red, the hair, the bone, all full exposed;
in shock, I begged the ambulance to come,
come quickly to my house to mend this girl
whose eye is now enwrapped in dripping blood.

I cried, "My rug is ruined! It was new!"
And all this small girl wanted was to build
a tower with the blocks my daughter had.
But now her face, distorted, must be sewn,
and likely will scar over, fully seen
above those big brown eyes, how obvious!

A mere hour later in the white-washed room,
her frame held tightly down on thin white sheets,
the doctor counted, "Breathe! One. Two. Three. Four."
—each count with needle point and binding thread.

My daughter, unrepentant, stood just near
the doorway, clad in curtains, barely there,
but in her hands a string, a bright balloon
shined by fluorescent lights a "Get Well Soon."

A Vision from the Past

He wandered through the willows wet with rain;
the sky above, thick haze, a streak, a stain
upon the landscape, darkening the vale.
His footsteps fell forgotten on the trail.

A filigree of droplets gathered, tears
shining, then the silver streaks appeared;
His blinking bent away the brackish beads,
then, falling from his cheek, a single please—

Could it be that, searching, he had found?
Or had he missed and lost the hallowed ground?
Could he hold that sunset in his palm?
Was that which sprung from lips a gentle psalm?

Recalling those days past, he closed his eyes,
and trusting in His Lord, he smiled then died.

Hasty Corporeal Ink

the ink is hypnotic,
a cohesion. its action
trickles—can recite
heartsick lacerations,
restrain reproach, can
incorporate painterly
phonic points.

shortly, the splotchy ink
is topical, a topsoil streak;
it hears, yet inept, ran,
and lost its torch—
recoils its ornate clarity.

contrary ink cools hot echoes,
halts sick snark
portrays close creations

From Flesh to Flesh

From flesh to flesh my body cannot bear
the ache of it—the frailty and loss,
gathered as a pool in pivots, joints
like gears, which grinding, squeal, approach the cross
and bow unworthy, lightened in its sight.
The terrors which His body bore that day:
the blood, the thorns, the nails, the screams, the gall,
His persevering power as He stayed—
opens a path for bearing my own cross.
I turn, I face the torturer herself,
myself whose cells despise my other cells,
and choose to live, again, with my own self.
But one day soon the flesh that pains me so
will bask in light of Christ's eternal glow.

After My Death

After my death, when all you will afford
is likeness of my image, young and fair,
I pray it will be hung and be ignored
as life continues on, no moment spared
to think upon my corpse deep in the ground,
awaiting resurrection. Though my smile,
immortalized, will beam from picture crowned
with ornate frame, it's simply a profile
of two dimensions, thus forevermore.
For those who know my deepest inner life,
remember me in passing, I implore—
yet think not on my suffering and strife.
Remember, love, how deeply we all yearn
to love and thus be loved, then, in return.

Afterword

Part 1: He informs dew.

Sunrise Sings is a Shakespearian sonnet.

He informs dew is an anagram of Proverbs 9:10–12, NKJV. Every letter used in these verses has been rearranged and put back together to form this poem, with no letters removed or changed.

Contemplating Life in the Conservatory is an ekphrastic pantoum. Ekphrastic poetry is inspired by works of art, and this poem is inspired by the painting *The Family of Mr. Westphal in the Conservatory* by Eduard Gaertner.

through vale and shallow height is an anagram-by-letter of Psalm 23, NKJV.

Forging a Sunset is a Shakespearian sonnet.

Startle— is an anagram-by-line poem. Every line in "Startle—" uses exactly the same letters as every other line.

Dusk is inspired by Germanic alliterative poetry and is constructed in the style of Caedmon's Hymn. Alliteration and kennings are major features of this style of poem.

Waxing Crescent is a Petrarchan sonnet and acrostic.

Insomnia is a series of haiku.

In the Wintertime is a rondeau.

Afterword

March in New York is written in alliterative verse.

Verdant is a meditation on the color green without mentioning "green." It's constructed using basic quatrains.

The Summer Storm that You Slept Through is a pantoum.

Autumn is written in free verse.

Fall Ends The left half of the poem is a Shakespearian sonnet in monometer following the rhyme scheme ABAB, while the right half—another Shakespearian sonnet in monometer—follows the rhyme scheme ABCB. Together, they form a Shakespearian sonnet in dimeter, with the terminal couplet remaining in monometer.

Unmoved Foundation is an anagram of Hebrews 4:12, NKJV.

The earth's loud weeping is a Shakespearian sonnet.

The Branch of Jesse Bears the Tree is a hymn, written as a meditation on Jesus bearing His cross.

The Fear of the Lord is the Beginning of Wisdom is a villanelle.

In Persona Christi is an ae freislighe poem. A traditional Irish form, it alternates between ending rhymes with three syllables and two syllables, with all the lines containing 7 syllables. It begins and ends with the same phrase, called a "dunadh."

A Firstborn Son is constructed using Sicilian quatrains.

Dear Peter is constructed using the "snowball technique" which was popularized by OuLiPo (an acronym formed from the name Ouvroir de Littérature Potentielle). This "Workshop for Potential Literature" was a group founded in 1960 by writer Raymond Queneau and mathematician François Le Lionnais. A traditional snowball poem increases each word by one letter. For example, 1, 2, 3, 4. "Dear Peter," however, increases by one letter in each line, then pushes out and down by expanding the number of letters in each word by line as well:

Afterword

1, 2, 3, 4, 5 / 2, 3, 4, 5, 6.

John 8:36 is a villanelle.

The Second Coming is a new form of my own devising wherein a "code" word becomes the organizing principle of the poem. In this case, the word "perfect" is both an acrostic, with each letter beginning each line, and the word which cycles through each line of the poem.

P E R F E C T
E R F E C T P
R F E C T P E
F E C T P E R
E C T P E R F
C T P E R F E
T P E R F E C

In this organization, each of the seven lines have seven words. Seven is the number of perfection in Scripture, which underscores the point: when Jesus returns, all will be perfect.

Part 2: Death is swallowed up in victory.

Late Nights with You is a villanelle.

It didn't have to be this way. is a Shakespearian sonnet.

Upon hearing his father died is written in blank verse.

The Ruins of the Monastery at Oybin is an ekphrastic sestina inspired by the painting *Gothic Windows in the Ruins of the Monastery at Oybin* by Carl Gustav Carus.

From Ashes to Ashes, Through Water and Fire is written in the style of a traditional Persian song.

Let Your Requests Be Made Known to God is an anagram-by-letter of Philippians 4:6–7, NKJV.

Mourning is a hay(na)ku.

Afterword

She always said lilacs were her favorite is a constructed of two decasyllabic quatrains, using the rhyme scheme AABB.

Inheritance follows a loose structure based on "As I" and "I . . . her."

Wishful Dreaming is written using quatrains using an ABCB rhyme scheme. This particular style of quatrain was my mother's favorite way to write her own poems.

The Tornado is a sestina.

Abishag the Shunammite is constructed using chiasm.

Death is swallowed up in victory is an anagram of 1 Corinthians 15:54, NKJV which is known for the title's phrase.

When my grandchildren ask me what the pandemic was like, I'll say: is a Shakespearian sonnet.

Part 3: Memory.

After the Storm is an ekphrastic terza rima inspired by the painting *After the Storm*, formerly attributed to Albert Bierstadt.

accelerate is a double acrostic, with the acrostic on the right side moving from bottom to top.

since feeling was first is written in the style of/after e e cummings' well-known poem "since feeling is first." Instead of meditating on the assumption that feeling first is necessarily better, is it true that "who pays attention to the syntax of things will never wholly kiss you"?

Leaving is written in a form of long meter, 10/8/10/8 syllable counts, with an ABAB rhyme scheme.

Her smile, then tears is an anagram poem. Each stanza begins with a new line, which is then anagrammed to create the rest of the stanza. Each line in each stanza uses exactly the same letters.

Memory is written in common meter.

Afterword

Unreal is a palindrome-by-word poem; it can be read both forward and backward by word.

The Look is a conversation poem, with the left side and the right side weaving together to make three poems in one: left poem, right poem, and both taken together.

Studying is a nonet.

Watching Time is written in free verse.

January Eighteenth is a lipogram about breastfeeding using only letters in the title: *j, a, n, u, r, y, e, i, g, h, t*. January 18 is the date on which both of my sons were born.

Son of My Right Hand is a Shakespearian sonnet.

Elegy is a cascade poem wherein each line in the first stanza becomes the terminal lines in subsequent stanzas. Line one becomes the final line in stanza one, and line two becomes the final line in stanza two, and so on. This poem is also an elegy, but not a traditional one; instead of mourning a person, this poem wrestles with mourning the loss of sleep.

NYE, NY, NY is written loosely in blank verse.

Recipe for a Failed Friendship is a variation on a list poem, reconceived as a recipe.

Grandpa, the Deep Sea Diver is a Shakespearian sonnet.

Recess is a Shakespearian sonnet.

Sandy Hook is a villanelle.

Can Houses Die by Suicide? is a Shakespearian sonnet.

Like Mother, Like Daughter is written in basic quatrains with an ABCB rhyme scheme.

In a boat not my own is a Shakespearian sonnet.

Part 4: Form and Function

Afterword

Form and Function is a lipogram using only the letters in the title: *f, o, r, m, a, n, d, u, c, t, i*.

Insatiable is a lipogram using the letters of the title: *i, n, s, a, t, b, l, e*.

un-mothering is an abecedarian poem that moves through the alphabet from beginning to end, then reverses and moves through the alphabet backwards. The switch in the middle of the poem also radically alters the meaning of the first half.

A Coarse Discourse is a Shakespearian sonnet in monometer, but it uses rhyming couplets instead of the typical sonnet rhyme scheme.

Gossip is constructed around letter numbers, with each stanza growing by one word and one letter per word. It grows as gossip spreads. This form is inspired by Greg Hill, who published a poem in this format on X (formerly Twitter).

do his hands cost less? is an anagram-by-letter of Psalm 82, NKJV.

masculine & feminine is a double acrostic, both beginning from the top. The left side says "masculine" and the right side says "& feminine."

Red Sunset is a ghazal inspired by the painting *Red Sunset* by Arkhyp Kuindzhi (Arkhip Ivanovich Kuindzhi) (Ukrainian, born Russian Empire, Mariupol 1841–1910 St. Petersburg).

Get Well Soon is written in blank verse.

A Vision from the Past is a Shakespearian sonnet.

Hasty Corporeal Ink is an anagram of my full name, Lisa Kathryn Cooper. The poem is a lipogram using only letters from the title/my name: *h, a, s, t, y, c, o, r, p, e, l, i, n, k*.

From Flesh to Flesh is a Shakespearian sonnet.

After My Death is a Shakespearian sonnet.

Afterword

Thank you to the following publications for featuring poems that appear in this volume.

Penteract Press:

"January Eighteenth" appears in *The Book of Penteract* March 21, 2022.

"accelerate" appears in *The Book of Penteract* March 21, 2022.

Curator Magazine:

"She always said lilacs were her favorite" was published online on January 28, 2022.

Fathom Magazine:

"From Ashes to Ashes, Through Water and Fire" was published on May 11, 2019.

"Dear Peter" was published on April 1, 2021.

Ekstasis Magazine:

"Dusk" was published in issue 5 on October 28, 2019.

"Startle—" was published online on June 7, 2021.

Grand Little Things:

"Can Houses Die by Suicide?" was published online on November 17, 2020.

Adversus Press:

"John 8:36" was published online in volume 1 on January 1, 2018.

North American Anglican:

"He informs dew" was published online on September 23, 2022.

"Death is swallowed up in victory" was published online on December 16, 2022.

"The Branch of Jesse Bears the Tree" is forthcoming as hymn lyrics in the film *Remember*.

www.ingramcontent.com/pod-product-compliance
Lightning Source LLC
Chambersburg PA
CBHW061452040426
42450CB00007B/1325